The Unseen Pattern

Christian A. Dickinson

Title: *The Unseen Pattern*
Subtitle: *God's Rhythms in Time, Beauty, and the Gospel*
Written by: Christian A. Dickinson

Illustrations by: Learning Engineered LLC
Published by: Learning Engineered Publishing

Library of Congress Control Number: 2025943457
ISBN (Print): 978-1-965741-42-9

First Edition: 2025

Printed & Created in: United States of America
Text and Illustration Copyright © 2025

Learning Engineered Publishing is a division of Learning Engineered LLC and a subsidiary of Carpe Diem Unlimited Holdings, Inc.

LEARNING ENGINEERED
PUBLISHING

Dedication

To my beloved mother, Sharon—

who carried us through Florida's summers,

taught us to find God's beauty in sunrises,

and revealed the sacred joy of a childhood well-lived.

Contents

Introduction: The Patterns We Were Made For

From the first sunrise to the last breath, our lives are shaped by patterns we rarely notice.

The slow turning of the seasons.

The rhythm of a heartbeat.

The quiet dance of light and shadow across ordinary days.

For a long time, I measured life by productivity and control—trying to bend every outcome to my will. But *grace has a way of interrupting our illusions*. I've learned that you can defy God's design, but you can never control the consequences. And I've discovered that *surrender*, not striving, is where freedom begins.

Some lessons came through unexpected suffering—seasons of caring for others, of walking through grief, of letting go. But the more I paid attention, the more I began to see: *God wasn't absent in those seasons*. He was quietly inviting me to notice His unseen patterns.

Patterns of mercy.

Patterns of order.

Patterns of redemption.

They're everywhere—for those with eyes to see.

In a dream, I stood beneath the Northern Lights, their radiant streaks pulsing across the sky in a silent symphony of grace. In that vision, I saw how *Jesus weaves through the Old Testament*—a vibrant thread of redemption, from the Passover lamb to the suffering servant, tying every story into God's eternal rhythm.

This book is a journey through those patterns. Each chapter explores a rhythm written into creation and revealed in Christ. *These are not random ideas stitched together.* They are pieces of a greater design, a divine symmetry that reflects the Gospel itself.

Whether you're reading this with your Bible open or simply longing for a deeper way to live, I invite you to *slow down, breathe deeply,* and notice what's always been there. Beneath the noise, beneath the pressure, beneath the chaos, there is a rhythm.

God's rhythm.

Chapter 1

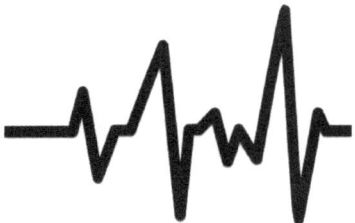

The Patterns We Live By

L ife hums with rhythms we rarely pause to hear—sunrises, heartbeats, community—each a note in God's redemptive song.

Genesis 8:22 promises: *"While the earth remains, seedtime and harvest, day and night shall not cease."*

Sin disrupts this harmony—grief, anger, loss—but Christ restores it. Psalm 51:10 pleads, *"Create in me a clean heart, O God,"* a cry answered in Jesus.

This chapter traces three rhythms—sunrise, heartbeat, community—inviting us into His purpose, even when life feels broken.

The Rhythm of the Sunrise

Each dawn keeps God's covenant, its light breaking the dark.

In Orlando, as a teenager wrestling with purpose, I watched the sky blush pink over palmettos, my heart heavy with family tension.

Genesis 8:22 reflects God's steady order, sustaining life through earth's 23.5-degree tilt. That sunrise, warm against my tear-streaked face, whispered renewal, echoing Revelation 22:5: *"There will be no more night."*

When grief lingers—a lost job, a fractured bond—Christ's dawn promises redemption, His return the final sunrise.

The Heartbeat's Cadence

Our heartbeat, pulsing over 100,000 times daily, carries God's rhythm within.

In a Lowcountry church, I stood among worshippers, their prayers rising like a pulse despite hidden sorrows—a mother's illness, a son's absence.

Psalm 51:10 seeks a restored heart, fulfilled in Jesus' sacrifice.

After a Florida hurricane, I shared coffee with a neighbor amid splintered trees, his kindness a heartbeat of mercy.

That moment, born of loss, revealed Christ's steady love, sustaining us through every storm.

The Pattern of Community

Community weaves us into God's purpose.

One Lowcountry evening, I joined a marsh-side picnic, strangers sharing shrimp and stories, laughter a hymn of unity.

Acts 2:46–47 shows believers breaking bread, reflecting Christ.

When neighbors rebuilt a fence post-storm, old rifts healed, fulfilling Ephesians 2:14: *"He himself is our peace."*

In my mentoring years, guiding students through doubts, I saw community bind broken hearts.

Sin divides, but Jesus restores, His cross uniting us in love.

The Gospel's Harmony

The Gospel weaves every rhythm into redemption, from Genesis 3:15's promised Savior to Revelation's new creation.

Jesus, the Word (John 1:3), restores what sin breaks.

In Orlando, my father's *Micah 6:8* hymn shaped me; in the Lowcountry, a fisherman's trust mirrored it.

C.S. Lewis wrote that creation's order reflects God's character.

When life feels off-key, the Gospel assures us: Christ's cross harmonizes every moment, inviting us to His song.

Invitation to Notice

Pause to see a rhythm—sunrise's glow, your heart's thrum, a friend's kindness.

Ask: *Lord, where is Your harmony?*

Gather on a porch to share a moment—a sunrise, a kind act—that reveals Jesus (John 8:12).

Journal a time His rhythm shone through pain.

Sketch a symbol—a sun, a heart—to recall His presence.

Create a keepsake—a pebble with *Psalm 51:10* written on it.

Read *Ephesians 2:14–16*: How is Jesus restoring peace?

These acts tune you to His song.

Closing Reflection

God's rhythms pulse through creation, binding us to Jesus.

That tearful dawn, those shared prayers, that rebuilt fence taught me His purpose.

Scripture reveals Him as the Composer who redeems every note.

As we turn to creation's music, may you notice His rhythms, trust His hand, and live the harmony you were made for.

Chapter 2

The Eternal Song of Music

Music is God's gift—a harmony woven into creation, resonating like a tide's pulse or a star's whisper. From a sparrow's trill to a soaring chorus, it echoes Jesus, creation's source (John 1:3).

In a world shadowed by pain—grief, fear, loss—music restores what sin disrupts. Psalm 40:3 proclaims: *"He put a new song in my mouth, a song of praise to our God."*

This chapter traces music's eternal harmony—through creation, human voices, and community—each note inviting us to hear Christ's melody, even in silence.

Music in Creation

Creation hums with God's symphony, older than time. One Lowcountry evening at dusk, I stood by a marsh, hearing herons' lilting calls and fiddler crabs' percussive scuttle. Science calls birdsong acoustic patterns, but its beauty sings of the Creator.

Psalm 96:11–12 declares: *"Let the heavens rejoice, let the earth be glad... let the fields be jubilant."* That marsh became a choir, each note echoing Jesus, the Word who spoke it into being.

When grief silences us, creation's melody whispers hope, reminding us *God still sings*.

The Human Voice

While creation hums, the human voice—*flawed yet holy*—carries God's song into our pain.

In a weathered New England chapel, a choir's trembling *Be Thou My Vision* rose as one prayer, blending sorrow and wonder. Augustine said music lifts us beyond words, stirring the soul toward God.

On a New Orleans street, a busker's raw *How Great Thou Art* slowed passersby, her unpolished voice a glimpse of Christ's compassion. Psalm 40 promises a *new song*, and in suffering, even a hum becomes a lifeline, drawing us to Jesus' nearness.

The Song of Community

Community amplifies music's power, weaving strangers into worship.

One night on Cocoa Beach, a rocket's fiery arc lit the sky, and an old man hummed *Great Is Thy Faithfulness*. Strangers joined, our voices blending under the stars.

Acts 16 tells of Paul and Silas singing in prison, defying despair. That beach became our sanctuary, our song uniting us.

Sin divides—pride, envy—but Jesus restores harmony, as Ephesians 5:19 urges: *"Sing and make music from your heart to the Lord."* In sorrow, *communal song binds us in hope.*

The Gospel's Melody

The Gospel is the harmony beneath all songs—from Genesis' promise to Revelation's praise—with Jesus' life and cross resolving every dissonance (John 1:3).

In my Orlando childhood, my father's guitar strummed *Micah 6:8—do justice, love mercy, walk humbly*—shaping my faith. On Cocoa Beach, that stranger's hymn turned a fleeting moment into worship.

C.S. Lewis wrote that music foreshadows heaven's joy. When our song falters, *Christ's melody carries us*, fulfilling Psalm 40:3: *"He put a new song in my mouth."*

Invitation to Sing

Pause to hear God's music—a bird's call, a hymn, your own breath. Ask: *Lord, what are You singing to me?*

Gather with friends on a porch or by a marsh to sing a hymn like *Amazing Grace* or *Be Thou My Vision*. Journal a moment when music drew you to Jesus, even in pain. Sketch a symbol—a note, a wave—to recall His presence. Create a keepsake—a shell with *Psalm 40:3* written on it.

Read *Ephesians 5:19*: How can His melody shape your day?

These acts attune your heart to His song.

Closing Reflection

Music is God's eternal harmony, resonating through creation and our fragile lives, *binding us to Jesus even when we're silent.*

That marsh at dusk, the chapel's choir, the beach's hymn—they taught me to *listen for His voice*. Scripture reveals Him as the *Composer weaving beauty from brokenness*.

As we turn to creation's spirals next, may you hear His melody, trust His song, and *live the harmony you were made for*.

Chapter 3

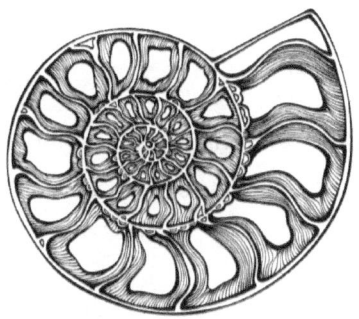

The Spiral of God's Art

Creation is God's canvas, its spirals—from seashells to galaxies—bearing His wisdom. Each curve reflects Jesus, through whom all was made (John 1:3).

Proverbs 8:27–29 sings of Wisdom's presence when God "set the heavens in place... marked out the foundations of the earth."

Yet sin mars this artistry—grief, pride, fear—obscuring the beauty we were meant to reflect.

This chapter traces creation's spirals—nautilus shells, sunflower seeds, woven baskets—each revealing Christ's redemptive design, even in our brokenness.

The Nautilus' Dance

The nautilus shell spirals in golden proportion, each chamber expanding at 1.618, a ratio echoing through art and nature.

Proverbs 8:28 says God "fixed securely the fountains of the deep."

In the Florida Keys, I held a nautilus shell, its delicate weight steadying me after a season of loss—a job gone, a dream deferred.

Its perfect curve whispered: God's design grows outward, never collapsing, holding even our grief.

That shell, warmed by my trembling hands, mirrored Christ's patient redemption, shaping beauty from pain.

The Sunflower's Pattern

Sunflowers radiate God's intricate beauty, their seeds spiraling in Fibonacci sequences—1, 1, 2, 3, 5, 8.

Psalm 19:1 proclaims: *"The heavens declare the glory of God; the skies proclaim the work of his hands."*

In a Kansas field, I stood among towering sunflowers, their faces tracking the sun.

After a friend's betrayal, their quiet order felt like a sermon, healing my cynicism.

Each seed, placed with care, reflected Jesus, the Word who orders all things, assuring me: no wound is beyond His artistry.

The Woven Basket's Loop

In North Carolina's Blue Ridge Mountains, I watched an artisan weave river cane into baskets, her hands following the material's spiral.

"It knows its shape," she said.

Colossians 1:17 declares: *"In him all things hold together."*

When my plans unraveled—a move I resisted, a future uncertain—her words lingered.

I traced the basket's loops, seeing God's hands weaving my story.

Like Christ's cross, which holds every broken thread, those loops taught surrender, revealing beauty in yielding to His design.

The Gospel's Artistry

The Gospel is the spiral redeeming all creation, from Genesis' promise to Revelation's new heaven and earth.

John 1:3 reveals Jesus as the Word shaping every pattern, His cross restoring what sin distorts.

In the Keys, the nautilus taught patient growth; in Kansas, sunflowers showed intimate care; in the Blue Ridge, baskets revealed surrender.

C.S. Lewis wrote that creation's order hints at a mind both vast and near.

When life frays, the Gospel assures us: Christ's artistry weaves every moment into redemption.

Invitation to See

Pause to touch a spiral—a pinecone, a fern, a swirl in your coffee.

Ask: *Lord, how is Your artistry shaping me?*

Gather with friends by a field or table to share a moment when God wove beauty from brokenness.

Journal a time His design surprised you.

Sketch a spiral—on paper or in sand—to reflect His purpose.

Create a keepsake—a shell with *Colossians 1:17* written beside it.

Read *Proverbs 8:22–31*: How is Jesus holding your life together?

These acts tune your heart to His craft.

Closing Reflection

God's spirals are His art, whispering redemption amid chaos.

That nautilus, those sunflowers, that woven basket taught me to trust the Artist's hand.

Scripture reveals Jesus as the Word who holds every thread, weaving beauty from our pain.

As we turn to water's life-giving flow, may you see His designs, rest in His purpose, and live the artistry you were made for.

Chapter 4

The Hidden Currents of Water

Water flows through Scripture and creation, shaping valleys and nourishing life as a symbol of God's presence and promise—from Genesis' rivers to Revelation's crystal sea. Jesus called Himself *Living Water* (John 4:14), a well that never runs dry.

Yet sin mars this blessing—floods destroy, droughts starve, thirst reveals our need.

This chapter traces water's hidden currents—streams, tides, rain—each a glimpse of Christ's life flowing into our broken places.

The Stream's Quiet Course

A stream carves paths through rock and soil, carrying life quietly.

In North Carolina's mountains, I sat by a narrow creek slipping between mossy stones, its unremarkable trickle shaping the valley unnoticed. Geologists say streams reshape the land grain by grain.

Psalm 46:4 proclaims: *"There is a river whose streams make glad the city of God."*

Even when life feels stalled—prayers echoing without reply—the stream's persistence reflects the Spirit's quiet work, *never hurried but always moving.*

The Tide's Relentless Pull

While streams show persistence, tides reveal God's relentless renewal. Twice daily, they advance and recede, pulled by the moon's unseen force.

One evening on Jekyll Island, I stood ankle-deep in the incoming tide, watching waves erase footprints in the sand—a parable of mercy washing the past clean.

Job 38 asks: *"Who shut up the sea behind doors?"*

In that salt-scented dusk, the tide's rhythm spoke of grace, unstoppable and sure—*cleansing regret, shame, and failure.*

The Rain's Gentle Benediction

Rain falls without prejudice, softening earth and awakening seeds.

In Orlando, after weeks of drought, summer rain tapped roofs and leaves, a thousand tiny blessings. Zechariah 10:1 urges: *"Ask the Lord for rain in the springtime."*

One afternoon, I saw a neighbor catch drops in buckets under leaky eaves, his gratitude treasuring each one.

When faith feels brittle, rain whispers abundance: *God sees, provides, restores.*

The Gospel's Wellspring

The Gospel is the wellspring cleansing all waters—flowing from Eden's river to the well at Sychar, where Jesus promised Living Water that satisfies forever (John 4:14). His cross pours out mercy, washing every sin.

In North Carolina, the stream taught quiet faithfulness.
On Jekyll Island, the tide showed relentless grace.
In Orlando, rain revealed unannounced provision.

C.S. Lewis wrote that water echoes the *River of Life*. When life dries up, the Gospel assures us: *Christ's fountain never fails.*

Invitation to Drink

Pause to notice water—rain on a window, a faucet's trickle, the tide's pull. Ask: *Lord, how are You quenching my thirst?*

Sit with friends on a porch or by a stream to share a moment when God refreshed your spirit. Journal a memory of grace like unexpected rain. Sketch a symbol—a droplet, a wave—to recall His faithfulness. Create a keepsake—a stone with *John 4:14* written on it.

Read *Revelation 22:1–2*: How is Jesus offering Living Water today?

These acts open your heart to His current.

Closing Reflection

Water is God's hidden current—a symbol of mercy flowing to the thirsty.

The mountain stream, rising tide, and summer rain taught me to trust His provision. Scripture reveals Him as the *Fountain who never runs dry.*

As we turn to light and shadow's dance next, may you drink deeply, trust His abundance, and *live the life you were made for.*

Chapter 5

The Dance of Light and Shadow

L ight pierces darkness, revealing God's presence amid life's shadows. Jesus declares in **John 8:12**, *"I am the light of the world. Whoever follows me will never walk in darkness."*
Sin casts shadows—fear, doubt, despair—but Christ's radiance restores hope.

This chapter traces light's rhythm—guiding, sheltering, illuminating—each a movement in God's dance, leading us to the cross where shadows are redeemed.

The Flame That Guides

God's light leads through uncertainty. In **Exodus 13:21**, a pillar of fire guided Israel through the wilderness, a beacon in the night.

One evening in Ormond Beach, after a season of mentoring a struggling student through his parents' divorce, I stood by a campfire, its flames flickering against the dark. My own doubts—about impact, about faith—loomed heavy. Yet the fire's steady glow, warm on my face, echoed Christ's promise in **John 8:12**.

When fear obscures the path, Jesus, the Light, guides us, His cross the ultimate beacon.

The Shade That Shelters

Light also offers rest. **Psalm 121:5–6** assures us:
"The Lord is your shade on your right hand; the sun will not harm you by day."

In a Tallahassee backyard, I sat under an oak's shadow, exhausted from caregiving for my father-in-law as dementia stole his stories. My daughter, Darcy, climbed into my lap, her small voice singing a hymn.

That shade, that song, felt like God's embrace, a refuge from grief. Christ's cross casts a shadow of mercy, sheltering us when trials burn.

The Gospel's Radiance

The Gospel reveals Jesus as the Light who overcomes darkness (**John 1:5**).

At that campfire, guidance steadied me; under that oak, shade restored me.

C.S. Lewis wrote that we believe in Christ as we believe the sun rises—not only because we see it, but because it illuminates all else.

When shadows loom—loss, doubt, pain—the cross shines, redeeming every moment with His presence, promising a day when *"there will be no more night"* (**Revelation 22:5**).

Invitation to See

Pause to notice light—a sunrise, a candle's glow.
Ask: *Lord, how is Your light guiding me?*

Gather with friends by a fire or window to share a moment when Jesus pierced your darkness.

Journal a time His light brought hope.

Sketch a symbol—a flame, a cross—to recall His radiance.

Create a keepsake—a note with **John 8:12** written on it.

Read **Psalm 27:1**: *How is Jesus illuminating your path?*

These acts draw you into His light.

Closing Reflection

Light and shadow dance in God's design, revealing Jesus.

That campfire's glow, that oak's shade, that child's song taught me His nearness. Scripture names Him the Light who redeems every shadow.

As we turn to time's timeless rhythm, may you follow His guidance, rest in His shade, and live the radiance you were made for.

Chapter 6

The Measure of Time

T ime flows like a quiet river—steady and unstop-pable—each moment marked by God's purpose. Scripture names Him the *Alpha and Omega* (Revelation 1:8), beyond time yet entering our days with care.

Sin warps time into a burden—regret over the past, fear of the future, weariness now.

This chapter traces time's hidden rhythms—*seasons, hours, kairos moments*—each inviting us to trust Christ with every breath.

The Seasons That Return

Seasons turn—winter to spring, summer to fall—each cycle shaped by God's steadfastness.

One Montana spring, I watched snow melt into soil, green shoots rising slowly, proving life returns. Ecclesiastes 3:1 declares: *"There is a time for everything, and a season for every activity under the heavens."*

When grief feels endless, seasons assure us: *no sorrow lasts forever*. That thawing field whispered resurrection—a quiet certainty that *Christ renews all things*.

The Hours That Shape Us

While seasons show cyclical faithfulness, hours teach God's constant presence.

One summer afternoon, beside a hospital bed, I watched a clock's slow ticks, each heavy with worry. Yet in that waiting, I found God near, shaping me through ordinary moments.

Psalm 90:12 pleads: *"Teach us to number our days, that we may gain a heart of wisdom."*

Every hour—mundane or weighty—is a gift. In hospital rooms or quiet mornings, *His presence anchors us*.

The Kairos That Interrupts

Not all time follows clocks. *Kairos*—God's appointed moments—breaks into the ordinary with purpose.

One autumn evening in Washington, D.C., heavy with regret, I was stopped by a stranger's quiet encouragement—*grace unannounced and undeserved.*

Mark 1:15 records Jesus' words: *"The time has come... the kingdom of God has come near."*

Kairos is *eternity touching now*, a gentle interruption showing *God is closer than we think.*

The Gospel's Timeless Promise

The Gospel redeems time—*past regrets, present struggles, future fears*—through Jesus, who entered history and rose to sanctify every moment (Hebrews 13:8).

In Montana's fields, I trusted His seasons.
In hospital hours, I sensed His nearness.
In D.C., I glimpsed His timing.

C.S. Lewis wrote that the present is *where time touches eternity*. When life feels hurried or stalled, the Gospel assures us: *every second is His.*

Invitation to Trust

Pause to notice time—changing seasons, passing hours, sacred moments. Ask: *Lord, how are You meeting me now?*

Sit with friends around a table to share when God grew your faith through waiting. Journal an ordinary moment made holy. Sketch a symbol—a clock, a leaf—to recall His sovereignty. Create a keepsake—a stone with *Ecclesiastes 3:1* written on it.

Read *Psalm 31:14–15*: How is Jesus holding your times?

These acts help you rest in His timing.

Closing Reflection

Time is God's silent rhythm, an unfolding story written with care. *No moment is wasted, no season unseen.*

That thawing field, hospital clock, and kairos encounter taught me surrender. Scripture reveals Him as the *Lord of time*, holding our days from start to end.

As we turn to the *prophets' patterns* next, may you *trust His timing, receive His grace,* and *live each moment as His gift.*

Chapter 7

The Patterns in the Prophets

A cross Scripture's tapestry, the prophets weave golden threads, their voices harmonizing across centuries to proclaim Christ's redemption.

Far from scattered, their words form a divine symphony, revealing a God who writes history with purpose.

Numbers, echoes, and fulfillment pulse with His intent, pointing to Jesus, the Pattern's completion.

This chapter traces these prophetic rhythms—numbers, echoes, fulfillment—each a note in God's redemptive song.

The Numbers That Pulse with Purpose

Scripture's numbers are God's signposts, carrying divine intent.

Three days in Jonah's fish, seven circuits around Jericho, forty years in the wilderness—these foreshadow Christ's three days in the tomb, His Sabbath rest, and His forty-day testing.

Hosea 6:2 sings: *"On the third day he will restore us, that we may live in his presence."*

One quiet evening, poring over Hosea in a dimly lit room, I felt my doubts unravel.

These numbers weren't random; they were God's heartbeat, stitching history to resurrection's promise, assuring me no moment is wasted.

The Echoes That Never Fade

Prophetic words resound beyond their time, carrying God's enduring promise.

Isaiah 53:5 foretold a servant "pierced for our transgressions," His wounds healing ours—a prophecy fulfilled in Christ's cross.

Micah saw a Bethlehem-born ruler, Zechariah a king on a donkey.

Isaiah 55:11 declares: *"My word... will accomplish what I desire."*

In a Charlotte small group, reading Micah's promise under flickering lamplight, I shared a season of faltering faith.

A friend's quiet nod, her own hope stirred by ancient words, reminded me: God's promises endure, speaking life into our doubts.

The Fulfillment That Completes the Pattern

Jesus is the tapestry's center, every prophetic thread converging in Him—Isaiah's Lamb, Jeremiah's branch, Malachi's healer.

One afternoon under a Charlotte oak, reading Matthew 5:17—*"I have not come to abolish [the Prophets] but to fulfill them"*—I saw history's design unfold.

When my father-in-law's dementia deepened, I feared loss would win.

Yet Christ's fulfillment, sealed on the cross, whispered hope: every prophecy points to a Person who redeems every broken moment.

Luke 24:27 reveals Jesus unveiling this on the Emmaus road, binding all Scripture to Himself.

The Gospel's Perfect Harmony

The Gospel weaves prophecy into one story: Christ's life, death, and resurrection fulfill God's plan.

That Charlotte oak became a sanctuary where ancient promises met my present need.

C.S. Lewis called the Old Testament a whisper of a Name.

When life feels fractured, the Gospel assures us: Jesus holds every thread, from Hosea's hope to the cross's victory, redeeming our stories.

Invitation to Trace the Pattern

Pause to read a prophecy—Isaiah 53, Micah 5:2—and see Christ within it.

Ask: *Lord, how are You fulfilling Your promises in me?*

Gather with friends by a fire to share a moment when God's Word stirred hope.

Journal a time His promise held you.

Sketch a symbol—a thread, a cross—to recall His faithfulness.

Create a keepsake—a slip with *Matthew 5:17* written on it.

Read *Isaiah 53:1–6*: How does Christ's fulfillment shape your trust?

These acts draw you into His purpose.

Closing Reflection

The prophets' voices are God's symphony, rising to proclaim salvation.

That lamplit study, that oak's shade, that shared hope taught me to trust His design.

Scripture reveals Jesus as the Author whose story never fails.

As we turn to the dance of our choices, may you trace His promises, rest in His purpose, and live the redemption you were made for.

Chapter 8

The Dance of Our Choices

O ur lives follow habits we barely notice—choices guiding our steps. Some align with God's purpose, leading to life; others entangle us in painful cycles.

Physics shows stars vibrating in harmony.
Nature reveals renewal's pulse.
But human decisions weave their own rhythms—*beautiful and flawed.*

This chapter explores the dance of our choices, why we repeat destructive cycles, and how the Gospel offers freedom to step into Christ's eternal purpose.

The Cycles We Repeat

Like the Israelites circling the desert, we revisit familiar struggles—anger, fear, regret—without knowing why.

In seasons past, I made choices I thought I could control, believing I could bend reality to my plans. I learned the hard way it doesn't work like that.

Dallas Willard wrote: *"You can choose to go against the natural order of things, but you cannot control the consequences."*

Romans 7:19 confesses: *"I do not do the good I want to do, but the evil I do not want to do—this I keep on doing."*

The Gospel invites us to *name these cycles* and surrender them to Christ.

The Choices That Build

While destructive cycles entangle, *faithful choices become holy ground*.

When my wife and I felt called to care for her father as dementia deepened, I was unprepared for the confusion and daily labor. Yet saying yes reshaped me.

God granted patience I couldn't muster, forging empathy as I sat through his repeated questions.

Galatians 6:9 urges: *"Let us not become weary in doing good, for at the proper time we will reap a harvest."*

That season's harvest was not ease but growth—a *deeper capacity to love.*

The Moment We Turn

Faithful choices lead to holy ground, but the most significant choice is to *turn back to God.*

Repentance isn't shame—it's *returning home.*

In caregiving, I faced temptations to escape into distraction or irritation, but turning to the small, faithful work brought God's presence near.

Joel 2:13 pleads: *"Return to the Lord your God, for he is gracious and compassionate."*

Turning is a daily step—*away from self, toward mercy.* Each return, however small, *aligns us with Christ's rhythm.*

The Gospel's Freedom

The Gospel redeems our choices, as Jesus rewrote human failure's ending.

"If anyone is in Christ, the new creation has come" (2 Corinthians 5:17).

In caregiving, I learned transformation isn't self-help—it's *surrender to the One who makes all things new.*

C.S. Lewis wrote that every choice moves us toward life or decay, but in Christ, *no path is too twisted to redeem.*

When we falter, *His grace invites us to step anew into His purpose.*

Invitation to Choose

Pause to notice your habits—those that build or break you. Ask: *Lord, what step are You calling me to take?*

Sit with friends on a porch or in a quiet room to share a pattern you feel called to break. Journal a time when a difficult choice shaped you for good. Sketch a symbol—an arrow, a seedling—to recall new beginnings. Create a keepsake—a slip with *2 Corinthians 5:17* written on it.

Read *Galatians 6:9*: Where do you need courage to choose faithfulness?

These acts guide you into His freedom.

Closing Reflection

Our choices are a dance—*sometimes clumsy, sometimes graceful*—but always full of possibility.

No habit is too strong for God's mercy to break. Caregiving's lessons, the pull of old cycles, and moments of turning taught me to *trust Christ's redemption*.

Scripture reveals Him as the *Redeemer of every step*.

As we turn to *suffering's hidden gift* next, may you *choose courage, trust His mercy,* and *live the freedom you were made for*.

Chapter 9

The Hidden Gift of Suffering

Suffering weaves through every life—*uninvited*, inter-rupting plans and testing faith.

Scripture affirms pain's reality, revealing what we truly be-lieve about God. Jesus, the *suffering servant*, entered our pain to redeem it (Isaiah 53:5).

Unlike the choices we shape, suffering often comes uncho-sen—yet God uses it to *refine, teach, and renew.*

This chapter traces suffering's hidden gifts—*refinement, de-pendence, hope*—each a space where Christ meets us in our deepest need.

The Refinement We Resist

Suffering exposes our illusions of strength and control.

One fall in Ormond Beach, I reached my limits—pressed by unfixable circumstances and unpreventable losses: a job's end, a fractured friendship.

1 Peter 1:6–7 compares trials to fire refining gold—*burning away what's false to reveal what lasts.*

That autumn taught me surrender, not striving, purifies faith. In pain's crucible—loss, failure, grief—God reshapes us, *forging trust stronger than before.*

The Dependence We Learn

While suffering refines, it also teaches *dependence on God's strength.*

Caring for my father-in-law in his final months brought a weight we weren't trained for—a shared sorrow for my wife, her sister, and our daughter as he slipped away.

2 Corinthians 12:9 declares: *"My grace is sufficient for you, for my power is made perfect in weakness."*

In those quiet nights, *God's presence carried us* when our strength failed, teaching reliance on His endless mercy.

The Hope That Grows

Suffering plants *seeds of hope*, even in barren seasons.

One Tallahassee evening, sitting on a porch after a season of loss, I traced stars above, feeling God whisper promises of renewal.

Romans 5:3–4 says suffering produces *perseverance, character, and hope.*

That porch became a sanctuary where pain birthed trust, not despair. When sorrow feels final, *God sows hope*, pointing to a future where *every tear is wiped away* (Revelation 21:4).

The Gospel's Healing

The Gospel enters suffering, with Jesus bearing wounds to heal ours: *"By his wounds we are healed"* (Isaiah 53:5).

In Ormond Beach, I learned surrender.
In caregiving, I found dependence.
On that porch, I glimpsed hope.

C.S. Lewis wrote that pain is *God's megaphone*, waking us to His presence. When suffering overwhelms, the Gospel assures us: *no pain is wasted*, for Christ redeems it all.

Invitation to Trust in the Dark

Pause to reflect on your pain—past or present. Ask: *Lord, how are You meeting me here?*

Sit with friends in a quiet place to share how God met you in suffering. Journal a moment when pain grew hope. Sketch a symbol—a star, a cross—to recall His presence. Create a keepsake—a stone with *Isaiah 53:5* written on it.

Read *Romans 5:3–5*: How is Jesus shaping you through trials?

These acts open your heart to His healing.

Closing Reflection

Suffering is God's unexpected vessel—*refining and renewing us*.

That autumn struggle, those caregiving nights, that starry porch—they taught me to *trust His nearness*.

Scripture reveals Him as the *Healer who redeems every wound*.

As we turn to *celebration's pattern* next, may you *trust in the dark, rest in His mercy,* and *live the hope you were made for.*

Chapter 10

The Pattern of Celebration

S uffering and joy weave together in God's tapestry, each a thread of His grace.

From Israel's feasts to Cana's wedding, Scripture reveals God's delight in celebration (John 2:1–11). Joy is not denial of pain but a defiant trust in His goodness, lifting us toward eternity.

This chapter traces celebration's rhythm—remembrance, thanksgiving, anticipation—each an act of worship echoing Christ's victory, drawing us to the cross's redemptive heartbeat.

The Remembrance That Grounds Us

Celebration begins by recalling God's faithfulness.

One Thanksgiving in Ormond Beach, we gathered around a worn table, hearts raw from losing my father-in-law. My daughter's small hand in mine, we shared stories of his laughter, tears mingling with gratitude.

Deuteronomy 16:15 commands: "Celebrate... because the Lord your God will bless you."

That meal, simple yet sacred, anchored us in God's past provision, grounding hope amid grief.

Remembrance, rooted in Christ's cross, assures us: His love endures.

The Thanksgiving That Transforms

While remembrance grounds us, thanksgiving reshapes our present.

One Atlantic evening, walking as the sunset spilled gold across the waves, I carried the weight of a fractured friendship. Yet gratitude—for the sky's beauty, a stranger's kind word—shifted my heart from scarcity to abundance.

1 Thessalonians 5:18 urges: "Give thanks in all circumstances."

My wife, Morgan, joined me, her quiet thanks for small mercies turning our walk into worship.

Thanksgiving, flowing from Christ's sacrifice, transforms even our darkest moments into gifts.

The Anticipation That Sustains

Celebration looks forward, trusting God's promises.

After a season of loss, I joined friends for a meal, their laughter and stories kindling hope.

Revelation 19:7 proclaims: "Let us rejoice... for the wedding of the Lamb has come."

That table, lit by candlelight, felt like a foretaste of eternity, where joy is unbroken.

John 16:22 assures us: "You will rejoice, and no one will take away your joy."

Anticipation, anchored in Christ's resurrection, carries us toward the cross's eternal victory.

The Gospel's Joy

The Gospel fuels celebration, as Christ's cross and resurrection secure unshakeable joy (John 16:22).

In Ormond Beach, remembrance rooted me.

By the Atlantic, thanksgiving restored me.

At that table, anticipation lifted me.

C.S. Lewis wrote that joy is the serious business of heaven.

When sorrow weighs, the Gospel points to the cross, where Jesus' victory ensures: no pain can steal His joy, which flows into every moment.

Invitation to Rejoice

Pause to name a joy, however small, and thank God.

Ask: *Lord, how is Your joy sustaining me?*

Gather with friends around a table to share a memory of God's faithfulness.

Journal a moment joy surprised you.

Sketch a symbol—a cup, a flame—to recall His goodness.

Create a keepsake—a card with John 16:22 written on it.

Read Psalm 100: *How does Christ's joy shape your day?*

These acts tune your heart to His celebration.

Closing Reflection

Celebration is God's rhythm, lifting us from pain to praise.

That Thanksgiving table, that golden sunset, that candlelit meal taught me to trust His goodness.

Scripture reveals Jesus as the Source of joy, His cross redeeming every sorrow.

As we turn to the cross's eternal rhythm, may you rejoice in His provision, give thanks in His presence, and live the celebration you were made for.

Chapter 11

The Rhythm of the Cross

Every rhythm we've traced—*sunrise, song, spiral, water, light, time, prophecy, choice, suffering, celebration*—points to a deeper truth: the *cross*.

Jesus is not merely a reflection of God's pattern; *He is the Pattern made flesh*, the Word through whom all things were made (John 1:3), the *suffering servant*, the *risen King*.

In Him, every note of beauty, shadow of pain, and act of surrender finds its *fulfillment*.

The Descent That Redeems

At the Gospel's heart is *descent.*

Philippians 2:6–8 sings of Jesus, who *"humbled himself by becoming obedient to death—even death on a cross."*

The world exalts ascent—success, control—but *Christ's rhythm is downward*, a love that empties itself.

One Good Friday in Tallahassee, I held my daughter's hand in a dim church, a bare cross draped in black. Silence carried grief, yet whispered mercy.

The cross is no accident; *it's redemption's pulse*, drawing sin into Christ's wounds to heal us.

The Rising That Restores

As dawn follows night, *resurrection follows crucifixion*. On the third day, the tomb stood empty.

Colossians 1:17–20 declares: *"In him all things hold together... through his blood, shed on the cross,"* He reconciles all things.

The cross and empty tomb restore what sin breaks—*time, beauty, breath.*

One Easter morning by the Atlantic, my daughter chased waves as the sun rose, laughter echoing after a friend's loss.

Resurrection isn't just history; it's eternity's heartbeat, making all things new.

The Pattern That Holds Everything

The cross unites every rhythm:

- **Sunrise** heralds resurrection.

- **Heartbeats** echo His broken body made whole.

- **Spirals** unfold life from death.

- **Songs** resound with His victory.

- **Water** flows from His side.

- **Light** pierces darkness.

- **Time** is rewritten by His love.

- **Prophets** foretold Him.

- **Choices** find mercy in Him.

- **Suffering** is held in His wounds.

- **Celebrations** draw from His joy.

Christ doesn't fit our rhythms; *He redeems them—turning pain to purpose, silence to song, death to life.*

Invitation to Surrender

Pause at the cross—in prayer or quiet. Ask: *Lord, what in me needs Your redemption?*

Sit with friends to share a moment when Christ met you in pain. Journal a time surrender brought peace. Sketch a symbol—a cross, a tomb—to recall His sacrifice. Create a keepsake—a slip with *Philippians 2:8* written on it.

Read *Isaiah 53:4–6*: How is Jesus carrying your burdens?

These acts draw you into His rhythm.

Closing Reflection

The cross is *creation's heartbeat,* God's love made visible.

That Good Friday silence, that Easter laughter, those moments of surrender—they taught me to *trust the Pattern death could not hold.*

Scripture reveals Christ as the One who *suffered and sings over us still.*

As we close, may you *rest in the rhythm of the cross—redeemed, restored, forever loved.*

Chapter 12

Conclusion: The Composer of Every Rhythm

I f you've read this far, know this: *You are not here by accident.*
Your life—*beautiful and broken*—is held in God's capable hands.

From sunrises to songs, spirals to suffering, the rhythms in these pages reveal a Creator *weaving redemption through every moment.*

Colossians 1:17 declares: *"In him all things hold together."*
In joy or pain, *every note of your story sings of Christ*, the Composer who makes all things new.

These chapters traced His handiwork:

- Sunrises whispering renewal

- Music stirring hope

- Spirals revealing artistry

- Water flowing with mercy

- Light piercing darkness

- Time unfolding purpose

- Prophecies converging in truth

- Choices shaping faith

- Suffering forging trust

- Celebrations lifting us to joy

- And the cross uniting them all.

Each rhythm—*ordinary yet sacred*—points to Jesus, who entered our chaos to redeem it.

On an Orlando porch, I once watched dawn break after a sleepless night, feeling His presence in the quiet light. That moment, like every story shared here, *taught me to trust His mercy*.

Scripture reveals a God who is *both vast and near*, patient with our questions, relentless in His love.

C.S. Lewis wrote that the world's beauty is a *glimpse of the One who made it.*

When life feels scattered, *His rhythms remain*—steady, purposeful, redemptive.

The Gospel assures us: *no moment is wasted, no pain beyond His reach, no joy apart from His heart.*

Invitation to Live in His Rhythm

Pause to notice God's rhythms around you—sunrise's glow, a song's echo, a kind act. Ask: *Lord, how are You weaving my story today?*

Gather with friends—on a porch, by a fire—to share a moment when you saw His hand.
Journal a rhythm that stirred your faith.
Sketch a symbol—a cross, a wave—to recall His love.
Create a keepsake—a stone with *Colossians 1:17* written on it.

Read *Revelation 21:5*: How is Jesus making your life new?

These acts attune you to His eternal song.

Closing Prayer

Lord,

You are the *Composer of every rhythm*, the *Author of every story*. Thank You for weaving beauty from our brokenness, redemption from our pain.

Help us notice Your patterns, trust Your purpose, and live Your joy.

May we walk in Your light, sing Your song, and rest in Your love—*now and forever*.

Amen.

Scripture Index

Psalm 139:16 – Introduction, Opening, Invitation to Begin: Every day ordained by God

Proverbs 8:22–31 – Chapter 3, Invitation to See: Wisdom's presence in creation

Proverbs 8:27–29 – Chapter 3, Opening: God's wisdom shaping the cosmos

Proverbs 8:28 – Chapter 3, The Nautilus' Dance: God's order reflected in the sea

Isaiah 53 – Chapter 7, Invitation to Trace the Pattern: Prophecy of the suffering servant

Isaiah 53:4–6 – Chapters 7 & 9, The Gospel's Perfect Harmony, The Gospel's Healing; Chapter 11, Invitation to Surrender: Jesus bearing our burdens

Isaiah 55:11 – Chapter 7, The Echoes That Never Fade: God's word accomplishing its purpose

Hosea 6:2 – Chapter 7, The Numbers That Pulse with Purpose: Third-day restoration pointing to Christ

Joel 2:13 – Chapter 8, The Moment We Turn: Call to repentance and return

Zechariah 10:1 – Chapter 4, The Rain's Gentle Benediction: Asking God for rain as provision

Matthew 5:17 – Chapter 7, The Fulfillment That Completes the Pattern, Invitation to Trace the Pattern: Jesus fulfilling the Law and Prophets

Mark 1:15 – Chapter 6, The Kairos That Interrupts: The kingdom's nearness in kairos time

Luke 24:27 – Chapter 7, The Gospel's Perfect Harmony: Jesus revealing how Scripture points to Him

John 1:3 – Chapter 1, The Gospel's Harmony; Chapter 2, Opening, The Gospel's Melody; Chapter 3, Opening, The Gospel's Artistry; Chapter 11, Opening: Christ as Creator, central to every rhythm

John 1:5 – Chapter 5, The Gospel's Radiance, Invitation to See: Light shining in darkness

John 1:16 – Introduction, Invitation to Begin: Grace upon grace through Jesus

John 2:1–11 – Chapter 10, Opening: Joy revealed at Cana's wedding

John 8:12 – Chapter 1, Invitation to Notice; Chapter 5, Opening, The Flame That Guides: Jesus as the Light of the World

John 16:22 – Chapter 10, The Anticipation That Sustains, Invitation to Rejoice: Unshakeable joy through resurrection

Acts 2:46–47 – Chapter 1, The Pattern of Community: Early believers sharing life

Acts 16 – Chapter 2, The Song of Community: Paul and Silas singing in prison

Romans 5:3–5 – Chapter 9, The Hope That Grows, Invitation to Trust in the Dark: Suffering producing hope

Romans 7:19 – Chapter 8, The Cycles We Repeat: The struggle to do good

2 Corinthians 5:17 – Chapter 8, The Gospel's Freedom, Invitation to Choose: New creation in Christ

2 Corinthians 12:9 – Chapter 9, The Dependence We Learn: Strength made perfect in weakness

Galatians 6:9 – Chapter 8, The Choices That Build, Invitation to Choose: Do not grow weary in doing good

Ephesians 2:14 – Chapter 1, The Pattern of Community: Christ as our peace

Ephesians 2:14–16 – Chapter 1, Invitation to Notice: Peace through the cross

Notes

The following citations provide sources for quotations used throughout *The Unseen Pattern: God's Rhythms in Time, Beauty, and the Gospel.* These references acknowledge the contributions of C.S. Lewis and Dallas Willard, whose insights enrich the exploration of God's rhythms.

Introduction, Opening: "You can choose to go against the natural order of things, but you cannot control the consequences." —Dallas Willard, *The Divine Conspiracy: Rediscovering Our Hidden Life in God* (San Francisco: HarperSanFrancisco, 1998), 15.

Chapter 1, The Rhythm of the Sunrise: "Creation's order reflects God's steady character." —C.S. Lewis, *Letters to Malcolm: Chiefly on Prayer* (New York: Harcourt, Brace & World, 1964), Letter 22, paragraph 13.

Chapter 2, The Gospel's Melody: "Music foreshadows heaven's joy." —C.S. Lewis, *Letters to Malcolm: Chiefly on*

Prayer (New York: Harcourt, Brace & World, 1964), Letter 22, paragraph 13.

Chapter 3, The Gospel's Artistry: "Creation's order hints at a mind both vast and near." —C.S. Lewis, *Mere Christianity* (New York: Macmillan, 1952), Book 1, Chapter 5.

Chapter 4, The Gospel's Wellspring: "Water echoes the River of Life." —C.S. Lewis, *The Last Battle* (New York: Macmillan, 1956), Chapter 16.

Chapter 5, The Gospel's Radiance: "We believe in Christ as we believe the sun rises—not only because we see it, but because it illuminates all else." —C.S. Lewis, *The Weight of Glory and Other Addresses* (New York: Macmillan, 1949), "Is Theology Poetry?"

Chapter 6, The Gospel's Timeless Promise: "The present is where time touches eternity." —C.S. Lewis, *The Screwtape Letters* (New York: Macmillan, 1942), Letter 15.

Chapter 7, The Gospel's Perfect Harmony: "The Old Testament is a whisper of a Name." —C.S. Lewis, *Reflections on the Psalms* (New York: Harcourt, Brace & World, 1958), Chapter 10.

Chapter 8, The Cycles We Repeat: "You can choose to go against the natural order of things, but you cannot control the consequences." —Dallas Willard, *The Divine Conspiracy: Rediscovering Our Hidden Life in God* (San Francisco: Harper-SanFrancisco, 1998), 15.

Chapter 8, The Gospel's Freedom: "Every choice moves us toward life or decay." —C.S. Lewis, *Mere Christianity* (New York: Macmillan, 1952), Book 3, Chapter 4.

Chapter 9, The Gospel's Healing: "Pain is God's megaphone, waking us to His presence." —C.S. Lewis, *The Problem of Pain* (New York: Macmillan, 1940), Chapter 6.

Chapter 10, The Gospel's Joy: "Joy is the serious business of heaven." —C.S. Lewis, *Letters to Malcolm: Chiefly on Prayer* (New York: Harcourt, Brace & World, 1964), Letter 22, paragraph 13.

Chapter 11, The Rising That Restores: "In Christ, all things hold together." —Paraphrase of Colossians 1:17; not directly attributed to Lewis or Willard but included for clarity as it aligns with the chapter's theme.

Conclusion, Opening: "The world's beauty is a glimpse of the One who made it." —C.S. Lewis, *Letters to Malcolm: Chiefly on Prayer* (New York: Harcourt, Brace & World, 1964), Letter 22, paragraph 13.

About the Author

Christian A. Dickinson is an author, speaker, and President & CEO of Learning Engineered Publishing, where he crafts faith-based devotionals, Bible commentaries, and children's literature. With over twenty years as a principal, teacher, and coach, Christian's passion for mentoring shapes his writing, inviting readers to see God's rhythms in life's patterns.

From a childhood prayer by a canal—answered with a fish that unveiled divine timing—to caregiving seasons that taught surrender, he finds God's redemptive heartbeat in sunrises, spirals, and the cross.

His works include *The Roar of 'Ēzer*, which celebrates women's God-given strength, and children's books co-authored with his wife, Morgan. Christian lives with Morgan and their daughter, Darcy, drawing daily inspiration from faith and family.

More by Christian A. Dickinson

I f you enjoyed *The Unseen Pattern*, you may also appreciate these Christ-centered resources:

The Curse of Time: Time Began When Eternity Broke
A theological and personal exploration of time as a consequence of sin—not a neutral part of creation. Drawing from Scripture, Church Fathers, and moments of divine encounter, this book challenges the assumption that time was God's original design and invites readers to rediscover the eternal now of God's presence.

Roar of 'Ēzer: Reclaiming God's Vision for Women's Strength
From Eden's garden to the early church, God named women *'ēzer*—rescuer, strength-bearer, equal partner in His image. This compelling biblical exploration invites women to rise, not as shadows but as co-laborers in God's kingdom. With Scripture, story, and a call to courage, *Roar of 'Ēzer* reveals

ipture, story, and a call to courage, *Roar of ʿĒzer* reveals that women were never meant to shrink. They were always meant to roar.

Jesus Was Funnier Than You Think: Unlocking His Wit, Wisdom, and Unexpected Humor
A fresh look at the wit and humor of Jesus Christ — revealing the brilliant, joyful ways He taught truth and disarmed pride.

Every Tear Remembered: God's Presence in Our Grief
A reflection on sorrow, healing, and hope through the lens of God's enduring love.

The Prophetic Equation: Thirty Prophets. One Christ. Zero Coincidence.
An exploration of how thirty prophetic voices across centuries, kingdoms, and crises converge with stunning precision in Jesus Christ — revealing that Scripture is not random, but a masterpiece of divine design.

Micah 6:8: A Prophetic Bridge to Jesus
A concise biblical commentary exploring how one ancient verse points forward to the life and ministry of Christ.

It's All or Nothing: How Jesus Raised the Standard from Tithing to Full Surrender
A biblical commentary challenging traditional views of

tithing by exploring Jesus' call to radical, Spirit-led generosity.

FULL CIRCLE: PREGAME — A Devotional Series for Athletes
Before the whistle blows and the lights come up, PREGAME challenges athletes to prepare their hearts as well as their bodies. With powerful stories, Scripture reflections, and real talk from the locker room, Coach Dickinson and Anthony "Diso" Paradiso equip competitors to lead with faith, play with integrity, and honor Christ in every moment.